A Few Words From The Artist

It was too tempting to let an opportunity go by without adding a word or two, as is my way. Regarding the really glowing words from friends and family (Editor's Note: see letters at back of book), I feel a little humbled and very flattered. Honestly, I did not hold them at ransom, (however, I have started speaking to them once again, now that they have written what I told them to). Of course I'm joking, and I would like to thank them for their input. Especially Alain, who did not mention what a roller coaster I am to live with sometimes, and very unpredictable. I can't thank him enough for his endurance and constant support.

I have met many Women during my six years in Canada, both at exhibitions and in my gallery, and it never ceases to amaze me the strength, perseverance, determination, tenacity, love and humour that I have been lucky enough to share with them. They are a strong bunch!

As we all know the advancing years catch us all up in the end, with good old gravity pulling harder, I don't think any of us think of ourselves as a '10' (or even a 5 and a half, if we ever did). The wonderful thing is though, we happily gain wisdom and realize that it doesn't really matter any more, and we are able to throw caution to the wind and laugh at ourselves and with each other.

I have often been asked, "Why do I paint fat ladies?" also, "Where do I find the models?" (that's a good one) and lastly, "Does anyone become offended?"

I paint well proportioned women, similar to the three wonderfully cheerful ladies that modeled patiently for hours at art college in California. I do not look for models, just sit in an airport, walk round a grocery store, sit on a park bench for a while etc,etc. No one has said to me that they are offended, in fact on the contrary, many ladies have told me that after looking at my paintings they feel so much more content and happy about themselves.

Since digressing from serious to humourous illustration during a stressful time in my life, I now have the opportunity to paint 'just for me'. However, when I witness the smiles and laughter on the faces of women, single or in groups, large or small, I feel absolutely great, and know that I have succeeded in something worthwhile.

To conclude, I feel my work is a celebration of Women, (along with the guys who appreciate the humour of it all). It is not to everyone's taste of course, and I wouldn't expect it to be, but keep your sense of humour if you can, as it may help you through a tough time as it did me.

Thank you to my loyal friends who keep coming back for more!

Wendy

© **Wendy Anne Klein**
Tickled Pink Studio
16392 Barkley Road
Lake Country, BC Canada V4V 1B4
Ph / Fax 250 766-1695
www.tickledpinkstudio.ca

ISBN 0-973-9107-1-2

Layout and printing by:
UBR Services / iPoDs *(Interior Print on Demand Services)*
1-10058 Hwy97N, Winfield, British Columbia Canada V4V 1P8
1-866-766-1098
info@ipods.ca • www.ipods.ca

For the Love of ^Real Women

by Wendy Klein

PARTY GIRLS

Who ever needs a reason
To party with some flare,
At any time or season
We really couldn`t care.

A chance to wear a slinky dress
Our makeup`s near perfection,
We left our office in a mess
No time for that correction.

These nice balloons took all our puff
That`s left us feeling lazy,
But now we`ve had some bubbly stuff
We`re getting wild and crazy

LADIES DAY FISHING

These four ladies have often been wishing
To find out just what they've been missing,
So they took out a boat
Though it seemed quite remote
They would seriously learn about fishing

They laughed with excitement and glee
As they mastered the art of the sea,
Being jolly and wise,
They soon improvised, and took home a large
Salmon for tea.

FOREVER FRIENDS

We've known each other many years,
Laughed a lot and shed some tears,
It only seemed like yesterday
I said goodbye and went away.

Our shopping days have sadly passed
Those sunny moments couldn't last,
But there will never be an end
To knowing that you're my best friend.

We're growing older day by day,
I really wish there was a way,
Without the cost of airfare booking
Just to see how good you're looking.

Well, at least to count grey hairs
To see how fast you climb the stairs,
And glasses - have you lost them yet?
You must have days when you forget.

And names of people that you meet
When walking daily down your street,
And do you leave your house not knowing
Exactly where the heck you're going ?

So even though we're far apart
I have you tucked into my heart
And phoning you will have to do
But honestly I still miss you...

AUTUMN LEAVES

Cooling breezes dusty sneezes
Winter's in the air,
Thoughts of childhood
Feeling so good
How I `d love to go back there

Crunching, kicking, wind`s a whipping,
Watch them fly and dance,
Let`s try to shed our "big girl" cares
And swing on every branch.

BIRTHDAY GIRL

Birthday girls find time to play
They never waste a minute,
An afternoon, a red balloon
Today the sky`s the limit.

BLOOMIN` LOVELY

Tousled hair and cheeks a glow
She watches all the tulips grow,
Shiny heads sway in the breeze
She brushes garden from her knees.

Her purple pants and tulips red,
A stunning sight it can be said,
But she must hurry can't you see
Her friends are coming round to tea.

CARE FREE

Carefree as the breeze in Spring
We sniff the swaying daffodil,
No thoughts of past or present cares
With my best friend this time stands still

CHANGE OF HEART

He ran amok with clumsy paws,
To scatter that noisy twittering mob,
Anticipation, sharpened claws,
To catch just one is such a job.

Rustling feathers flapping wings,
This happens every day,
It`s much too high, I`m coming down
They're not so tasty anyway.

CHIT CHAT

Blesséd is the cool night air
That brings relief from summer glare,
Neighbours taking time to pause
From cooking meals and dusty chores.

We live in quiet harmony
And days might pass when we don`t see
each other, when it`s this or that
which take our time from chit and chat.

CHRISTMAS CAROLLING

A woof and a bark
While heralds hark
In chilly air we croon,
White curtains quiver
While we all shiver
It feels like snow
Let's go home soon.

COCKTAILS AT SHASTAS

This really is unusual
So far up off the ground,
I don't see chairs and tables
As I start to look around.
This must be that new nightclub
It says so on the sign,
I think I need another drink
I'm sure that's pollen in my wine.

ENCHANTED EVENING

These two are dancing in the buff
It really can`t be beat,
It`s such a great idea I think
To overcome this heat.

They`ve had some wine the music`s on
The neighbourhood is sleeping,
What harm is this, but we just hope
That nobody is peeping.

FANCY DRESSERS

Furry bunny dressing funny
Clowning, masking ears a flop
Nose of red and fuzzy head
We like to be who we are not.

FANCY PANTS

Frosty bites on powdered nose,
Arms outstretched and head held high,
Just a whiff of perfume lingers
in the air as she glides by.

Bouncing breasts and perfect poise,
Fashion clothes one would desire,
Thoughts of slippers, cozy chair,
And sipping whisky by the fire.

GARDEN PARTY

Us ladies of the garden club
Are busy bees today,
We have a special function
And we really can`t delay.

Let's tidy up the garden
As it`s really quite a mess,
We`ll do it in our undies girls
Until it`s time to dress.

The tea we`ll serve in china cups
With sandwiches and buns,
We sent our invitations
But let's welcome all who comes.

These tulips need some elbow grease
They`ve grown so big and tall,
Come on ladies do your stuff
If we move fast we`ll clean them all.

GETAWAY

Lives too busy, makes us dizzy,
No time for chit or chat,
I want to shop and sip some tea
How do you fancy that?

GOSSIP

Did you hear what Mable did ?
She stayed all night with who?
That dress she wore at last years dance
I promise I won't tell, will you?

I saw your neighbour with a man
Yes half her age and dishy,
Your husband`s working late these nights
So don't you think that`s fishy?

HIGH TIDE

We love the cool tranquility
With toes a wiggling in the sea,
A good idea we have to say,
But mind you both don`t float away.

The day is warm we`ll take a nap
While cooling waters gently lap
Creeping slowly to our knees
If we don`t notice, whistle please.

LADY IN RED

It has to be said that the lady in red
With her flowers and moggy named Basil,
Should give you some cause
For a moment to pause,
And to realize your life's such a frazzle.

LONG WAY HOME

Bad boy Benny once again
You left your bed to roam,
It's taken hours to find you Puss,
Now we must take the long way home.

LUNCH DATE

We can`t wait
For our lunch date
This busy day
We`ll find a way
To share a smile
And shop a while,
Our late return
Will cause concern
But blame the weather
Stick together
After all....
Who knows what tomorrow holds
With rush of time as life unfolds

MIDNIGHT SNACK

I just had a lovely dream
Of last night's apple crumble,
Real enough to taste it still
That makes my tummy rumble.

I tiptoe down at 12 pm
Must mind the creaking stair,
Anticipating, licking lips
While thinking of what's waiting there.

PEACHY

We`ll take a few hours off today
And use this time for leisure,
We `ve worked a lot, so packed a bag
With goodies for our pleasure.

Our fellows have gone fishing
So we know we`ll have some time,
Let`s lay here in the sunshine
And finish off the wine.

PENNY FOR THEM

This lady moves with gracefulness
And pedals every mile,
With certain flare and elegance
She stuns you with her smile.
Her mog will ride behind her
As he plays a special role,
She tends to be a dreamer
So he'll often take control.
He also keeps her balance
Which to her has great appeal
As often she's distracted
And her dress will clog the wheel.

PIROUETTE

She loves to dance and has a chance
To practice every day,
She skips and trips, her tootoo flips
Her body starts to sway.

Her hungry mogg with eyes agog
Is watching from the corner,
"I guess I won't be fed right now
So why don`t I just join her".

Wal Klein

RETIREMENT PLAN "A"

He hated his job and confessed,
That his boss he`d begun to detest,
His thoughts were inspiring,
And dreamt of retiring
So made plans for a long deserved rest.

To his neighbour he`d sell his grass mower,
And his wife he would now get to know her,
She got quite excited and he was delighted,
While packing her fluffy pink boa.

All the sights in the desert he'd show her
As the pace of their life became slower,
But he had quite a fright,
When she danced every night,
Nearly naked, she was quite a goer!

SHAKIN` ALL OVER

We two ladies are well past our prime,
And we know it`s a terrible crime
To just sit and grow old,
So let`s start to be bold,
It`s a shame to waste any more time.

We began with a parachute jump,
But we both fell with a terrible bump,
So we started car racing
But found we were facing
Some real aches and pains in the rump.

Then one said "let `s be really courageous,
Belly dancing can be so contagious."
We soon started to find,
That with each bump and grind,
We became more and more quite outrageous.

SNOW BUNNIES

Bunnies giggle bottoms wiggle
Furtive glances through the snow,
Gently sipping, ice that's dripping,
Trendy outfits, quite a show.

We'd never make that moving chair
Before we had to pee,
And pulling ski suits on and off
Would sap our energy.

No puffs or groans nor aching bones
No injured arm or knee,
No thoughts of racing down that hill
We'll stick to après ski.

SWEAT SHOP

Huff and puff we stretch and strain
These antics make us giggle,
I `m not sure why we`re all so vain
Our bottom`s meant to Jiggle.

It really doesn`t matter if
Our bodies`s are not stunning,
Let's try to walk a bit each day
And quit this awful running.

My treadmill must be rusty now
And clothes are getting tight,
I want to eat that chocolate bar,
Temptations I will fight.

WEIGHING IN

Weighing in on Monday
In only underwear,
Can put you in a touchy mood
With feelings of despair.

Last Friday I seemed lighter
These scales have gone berserk,
I only ate three apple pies
This diet doesn't work !

WEIGHING IN AGAIN

I creep into the bathroom
And softly lock the door,
This time I`ll climb on slowly
Not just jump on like before.

I swallowed so much water
Until I thought I`d drown,
So if I take a tiny peek
That needle must be down.

A lettuce leaf at lunch time
Not sticky buns and jam,
So I deserve some chocolate now
And I don`t give a damn.

A CELEBRATION

These ladies got together
When the poppies were in bloom,
It may be someone's Birthday
One could easily assume.

With sweetness on their laughing lips
And sparkling wine that sings,
They celebrate the gift of life
Don't wait too long to do these things.

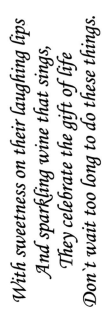

ANNIVERSARY WALTZ

We never miss this special day,
This year we feel quite daring,
While trying to coordinate
The clothes that we are wearing.

Tripping, dipping, swaying close
We dance with jubilation,
Our anniversary's here again
Come join our celebration.

BOOGY WOOGY

Boogy woogy, cha, cha, cha,
Us girls are really swinging,
I hope the neighbours don't complain,
Is that the doorbell ringing?

Come in and join us – have some wine
We'll get those hips a jiggling,
You'll feel the burn and trim your thighs
When everything starts wiggling.

CARRY CATS

Carry cats as you can see
Have worked it out so carefully,
Making out they're weak and soft
So owners lift them up aloft.
Fancy bags with flowery trim,
An aching arm endured by him,
Nothing matters don't you see
As long as we ride comfortably.
Fashion statements here and there,
Ride together we don't care
As long as we don't use our feet
And end up with a fishy treat.

CONDO CATS

Those lucky country cousins
Seem to do just what they please,
Hunting down the kitchen mice
Chasing birds in trees.
Their coats are wild and matted
We're brushed a lot its true,
But we still cough up furballs
And we're fussy eaters too.
Our life is very boring
So we scratch things with our claws,
We'd rather sniff the cool night air
Feel earth and grass beneath our paws.

CONNOISSEURS

*Our fashion is creative
and we hold our glass with style,
We'll sample every one you know
And smack our lips a while.*

*Perfected are our taste buds
With each nuance flavours burst,
It's near the end of Winefest
So we're very well rehearsed.*

*We ladies are discerning
And we like to take our time,
Our legs they may be wobbly,
But our mood is quite sublime.*

FRIDAY NIGHT

Is it your turn first and my turn next?
These weekly baths are so complex,
Let's both jump in and wine I'll fetch
And fill this tub up to our necks.

Washing toes and hard back scrubs
Will wear these soap bars down to stubs,
I wonder who builds bigger tubs
To hold this mound of squeaky suds.

HOT DATES

Twizzled hair and perfumed air
Warm anticipation,
Many hours of fluff and stuff
Need careful dedication.

Being late for this new date
Will cause us great distress,
Underwear and static hair,
This room looks such a mess!

Knobbly knees, eyebrow tweeze
Taxi cab needs booking,
Hoping this is all worthwhile
And my hot date's good looking.

LAP CAT

At 10 pm she felt so tired and rose to go to bed,
That meant removing Cedric who was draped across her head.
At 2 am she staggered to the bathroom for a pee,
Again disturbing Cedric who lay snoring on her knee.
At 8 am she made some toast and buttered it to eat,
But Cedric's paws stood firmly on her bunny slippered feet.
At 3 pm she crept upon the sunbed for a nap,
Old Cedric didn't take too long to curl up on her lap.
At 6 pm she felt his claws as Cedric had a knack
of knowing when the time had come to eat his evening snack.

MAKEOVER

I may have reached a certain age
My wrinkles they are few,
But when this icky pack comes off
I'll look as good as new.

I tell my mirror every day,
You really must expect it,
But damn it girls it's just not fair,
And I will NOT accept it.

A little to the left young man
Now don't you be too bold,
My skin was always silky soft
I hate this growing old.

It makes me chuckle, all's not lost!
These lines are not degrading,
For soon the process will reverse
As my eyes, they keep on fading.

Don't be cheeky fellow friends,
You think you are exempt.
I see some black hairs on your chin,
And my, you look unkempt.

MOONSHINE SOCIETY

Moonshine ladies meet at night,
The moon is full and that's just right
For dancing and for feeling free,
They're doing what comes naturally.

Fire that sparkles, faces glow,
It's not the wine I'm sure you know,
And not the moon that shadows cast
As toes dance softly on the grass.

To feel the breeze touch skin and hair
No one to judge why they are there,
Oh! How I wish to join those three
To dress and dance outrageously.

I'd grow my hair down to my knees
and wave my arms so gracefully,
These things will make it plain to see
That I've found ME quite totally.

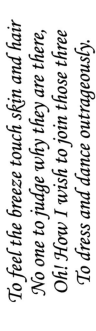

MS. OKANAGAN

A bevy of local beauties,
Provocative and chic,
In offices and stores we see them
Working all the week.

But when the flag is flying
And they line up side by side,
How difficult to pick one
Oh how does one decide.

Now they pose in swimwear,
Purple, yellow, blue and pink,
It's really quite a giggle
But it's harder than you think.

There's Mabel from the coffee shop,
She's done all this before,
Last year she won the title
And has followers galore.

But lets all keep it friendly
Whatever shape or size,
I think we know who'll steal the show
That pup will win the prize!

OKANAGAN BEAUTIES

You'll see them lying on the beach
Or walking down a sunny street,
They proudly hold their heads up high
These ladies you' would love to meet.

Their bodies soaking up the sun
Gentle breezes, ocean spray
Careful not to burn those parts
That they keep hidden every day.

PRIORITY ONE

The day is warm the grass is green
With latest style of clubs you've seen,
There's some who love to hit a ball
But some don't have that yen at all.

"You guys just go ahead of us,
We're not sure why you make a fuss,
We'll just have lunch here on our laps
And chat about our handicaps".

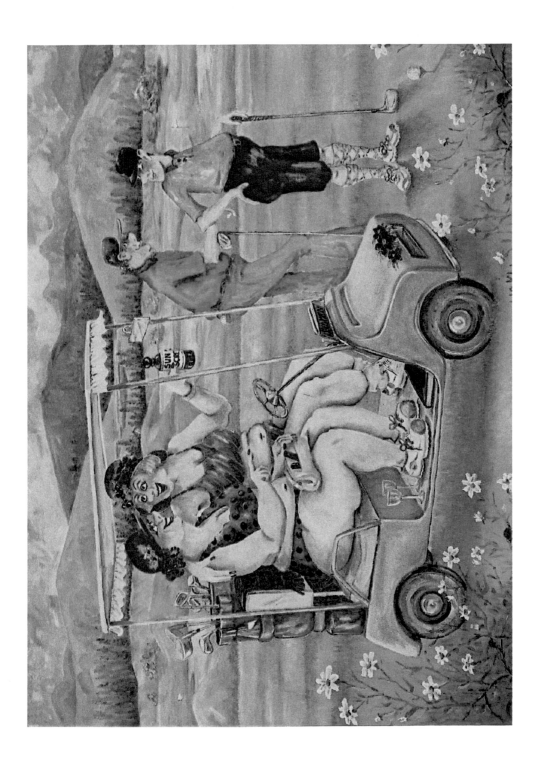

QUEEN OF HEARTS

It's Friday night and once again
  We gather for a game,
There's only just the four of us
  Each meeting just the same.

But recently there came to be
  A new face on the street,
The ladies were suspicious,
  But the guys thought she was neat.

They asked her round for cocktails
  And a game of cards for fun,
But she was one smart cookie
  As each game with them she won!

REMINISCING

Alas we have become of age,
As youth will never last.
So lets sit here and drink some tea
And talk about the past.

Remember all those funny clothes
We must have been insane,
We should have kept them all my friend
They've all come back again.

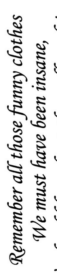

SCRABBLE

Old Mabel hasn't blinked at all
She's lacking concentration,
Those gin and tonics mixed with wine
Has caused inebriation.

I really think I'm losing ground
And Lilleth's always cheated,
So where are all those lovely nouns
One hates to be defeated.

With words like 'sat', 'bad', 'sad', and 'go'
Proved I would win I'd say,
But nothing seems to come to mind
Thats spelled with Z X J !

STILL CRAZY

What do they say about 'long in the tooth',
You're as young as you feel - don't they mention
If your heart still has wings
And you want to do things
That releases all life's stress and tension.

Let your hair become tangled and long,
When you're walking try whistling a song,
In each ear place a daisy
And act a bit crazy
If it feels good how can it be wrong?

Grubby knees, rosy cheeks, sense of fun,
Growing old we will never outrun,
Be an innocent child,
Let your feelings run wild
And pretend life has only begun.

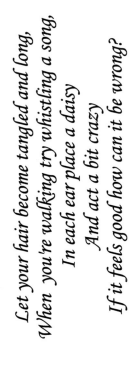

SWEET TOOTH

Yummy yum yum, yummy yum
Feel the sweetness on the tongue,
I'll have a bite I can't resist,
Now you taste mine I do insist.

We just ate lunch with French fries too,
A glass of wine … well, just a few
When evening comes we'll look so cute
What was that plan, to just eat fruit??

Telling jokes and laughing loudly,
Sunny smiles we sit here proudly,
Let's verify our master plan
To have a ball and get a tan.

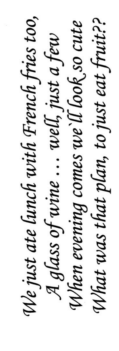

THE DIVOT

Us golfing girls are out again,
Our clothes the best design,
We must make sure we're looking good
So give us extra time.

We bought these fancy golf clubs,
New make up for effect,
But who will tell them at the club
The fairway's almost wrecked!

THE WEDDING

'Tis a grand affair
If you pass that way,
Through an English town
On a warm spring day.
The groom all spruced,
And the bride in lace,
When they join as one
You can see the face
Of a dear old aunt
With her bag of rice
As she sheds her tears
And kisses them twice.

TOUR DE FRANCE

Poor old Betty was in quite a state
When her bike couldn't carry her weight,
So she begged and she pleaded
And told them she needed
To ride in a more comfy state.

Because of her bulk and her size
The poor men were dropping like flies
So she made a suggestion
That seemed out of the question
By offering herself as first prize!

VOLUPTUOUS FAIRY

Centuries old these magic tales
And childlike sweet creations,
Fantasize with mystery
Your own imagination.
Through perfumed mist they rise and fall,
Alighting softly large and small
She's so beguiling, spirits lift,
When touched by her,
Your thoughts will drift.

WANTING ALL THE BEST CATS.

At last the morning's over with
The housework done and dusted,
I wonder where that moggy is
He really can't be trusted.
He has this awful habit of
demanding to be fed
and then he has audacity
to stretch out on my bed!

WILLPOWER

She baked a cake this morning,
Then covered it with cream,
And added one red cherry,
Just to make it look a dream.

It's making us feel crazy,
Why not move it out of sight,
But maybe we should test it,
Let's just take a tiny bite

WINNING STREAK

We started out playing Gin Rummy
But now it's becoming quite funny,
Old Bill's quite a Joker
He's changed to Strip Poker
And our chances of winning are crummy.

Our Mabel is far from a streaker
And her outlook is getting much bleaker,
With not much to go, before she will show
All she has, and that really will freak her.

Us ladies wore layers of clothes
Preparing for anything goes,
But that old man's cheating,
He takes some real beating
Still covered from his waist to his toes

A word about my Wife, from the "other half"

People ask me many times,"What is it like living with an artist like Wendy?" Well on reflection it would entail quite a number of descriptions and here are some. Her continuing concern for all members of her family, friends and others, the wanting to know, (constantly questioning). The appreciation of the beauty of every living thing, from the spectacular colours and hues of the setting sun to the intricate details of the smallest flower or insect. Wendy has many times brought me down to earth and made me realize the wonders of the simple life, the uncomplicated and innocent flow of how our daily routines should be.

There is no doubt that a creative mind can sometimes also be chaotic and surprising, which in Wendy`s case makes for an exciting and to say the least colourful lifestyle, this can sometimes be somewhat crazy but then this has taught me patience and endurance, something we all need in this life.

Wendy`s warmth, her love and concern for people and all things, her creativity, her humour and laughter and her ability to bring happiness into peoples lives, leaves a constant light in my heart, and for that, I love her and thank her.

Alain

From a Daughters perspective...

Under my bed, I have an over-sized, over-stuffed box full of memories from my childhood and all the years in-between. There's some trinkets, many special photos and tons and tons of notes and letters & colorful cards that my mom has written or drawn for me over the years. Each one has that special something...whether it be encouraging words, a limerick, or an amazing drawing to make me laugh...And each one deserves it's rightful place on my shelf. However, there could never be a shelf big enough or strong enough to hold them all.

I will always keep these mementos somewhere safe, though, and easy to reach... as I know laughter & love is the best medicine there is.

Throughout my life, my mom has taught me this..She has also taught me to be good, to be respectful, to be honest, to be loving & to be proud of who I am. And by diving into her brilliant imagination & using every ounce of creative talent, she delivers that same message through her art...Be proud! And laugh!! Out Loud!!!

I know I'm so proud of her... With every stroke of the brush her passion for life is released...and the inner-child speaks loudly...With every color from the rainbow she uses...the world becomes a more vibrant & happier place to be...

Philippa

"Hello Wendy… welcome to the Okanagan"

"They're here," I called to my husband Graham, as I flung open the front door to meet Alain, our oldest friend in Canada, and his new love Wendy Anne. Curiosity was killing me to see this 'wonder woman' we had been told about, who he was changing his whole life around to be with.

Was it yesterday or a hundred years ago that I first met my dear friend Wendy? There stood this slim middle aged woman, attractive but wistful, hesitant and even a little sad. I could see how nervous she was at meeting me, how awful she must have felt to be confronted with this blonde, loud, overconfident (overweight) woman standing in front of her, not knowing what reaction to expect. I put my arms around Wendy and said, "Hello Wendy, welcome to the Okanagan".

A year later Wendy had moved to Canada from France and we were spending a lot of time together, and by then we were lifetime friends. I had seen some of her work and I marveled that she had a great gift for colour, and her imagination was astounding. Her hidden sense of humour came out in full force in her fat lady paintings, and her humourous portrayal of everday situations is remarkable. The next step was to get Wendy to exhibit her work. I knew 'Art Walk' was to be Wendy's launching ground, so whilst driving through Winfield I pulled up in front of the registration office and told her to get her butt in there to sign up! The rest is history. 'Art Walk' was a great success, and as I stood back I watched my friend confidently talking and laughing along with the public who were seeing themselves and their friends in the comic situations that her paintings portray. Of course I am there, just as all women are, fat or thin, blonde or brunette, young or… 'mature' and we have all thought of ourselves as Wendy sees us.

My final words to Wendy are, "Thanks Wendy for being you. For giving us your talent, your humour, your gift.

Your forever friend Diane

When Wendy asked me to write something to be included in her book I was full of glee!!!! Now I have a chance to tell the world what I really think about her!!! I met Wendy at school, in England, where she was already known for her drawing ability, but we didn't become close friends until we both went to live in California. I was always astounded by her talent and by the diversity of her subject matter but when she began to produce the drawings of ME I knew she really had a gift!!! Each time I saw a new drawing, there I was, healthy happy and distinctly heavy. I know I had spent a lot a time with her but when did she see me bending over picking that flower? I had never played golf with her but there I was. Nobody had ever caught me having my midnight snack , so how did she know? Then I began to notice her Dad, my husband, her husband , friends, it was amazing. So here I am sprinkled all over a book! Look closely, you will see me. Or is it you? Or a friend, a relative? The only thing I can guarantee is that they will make you smile and sometimes laugh out loud. So thank you my dear friend, your artistic talent coupled with your amazing insight and ability to see humour everywhere has helped and healed so many. Now about that drawing with the whip……how the hell did you know about that?

Love Anne